Rise Up Be You

Shayla Humphrey

Artist was Natasha Faye

Website: www.peace-of-you.ca
Facebook: Shaylapeaceofyou
Instagram: PeaceofYou.Shayla
Email: Shayla.peaceofyou@gmail.com

CONTENTS

Chapter 1: Fitting In 1
Chapter 2: Conflict 6
Chapter 3: Safety 20
Chapter 4: Companionship 25
Chapter 5: Power Of Fear 29
Chapter 6: Life Lessons 32
Chapter 7: Forgiveness 39
Chapter 8: Signs Before The Gifts 43
Chapter 9: Courage 48
Chapter 10: The Shift 52
Chapter 11: Other Side 56
Chapter 12: Past Life 62
Chapter 13: Soul Connections 66
Chapter 14: Trusting Yourself 71
Chapter 15: Opening Doors 74
Chapter 16: Balance 77
Chapter 17: Future 81
Chapter 18: Dimensions 85
Chapter 19: Parents 89
Chapter 20: Roller Coasters 92
Chapter 21: Deeper Meaning 97

Acknowledgments

THANK YOU TO MY parents for not giving up on me. Thank you to Anil for believing in me and making this book possible. Thank you to my boyfriend who always supports my dreams, no matter how big they are. Thank you to the higher source that has always been present in my life and stretching me to grow.

Preface

THE PURPOSE OF THIS book is to bring awareness to mental health. It is a growing concern with a strong need of action to heal it and overcome it.

This is a story of true events. My intention is not to call people out but to call awareness the problems we face with our youth and bullying. *(Names have been changed to protect those involved.)* I am actually not a fan of the term bullying because people aren't bullies, people are souls and there are only moments of bullying behavior. We need to separate the two. The behavior has to stop; we have to find a kinder way.

The first part of this book is unedited as possible so that it stays true to the journal it was captured from. It evolves as I evolved.

I want to thank my creator for having faith in me and making me an instrument for peace.

CHAPTER 1

Fitting in

LIFE IS ANYTHING BUT normal. Yet we all strive to be normal and fit in. Most of us will do almost anything to be accepted. We will change how we look, change our friend group, even change how we act. We all need to feel significant and have a sense of purpose and belonging.

My life was anything but easy. One thing happened after another, for the longest time I thought there was something wrong with me. I became hopeless and did not want to live. I attempted suicide but life had other plans for me.

Let me start from the beginning of my journey. The following chapters are captured from my diary and journaling.

The first day of kindergarten is a time where we have to say goodbye to our parents for a whole day and be surrounded by strangers. We learn to sit in our desk, as we are told to be quiet and listen. For me listening was hard, I was born hard of hearing. My parents had no idea until my kindergarten teacher spoke to my parents and suspected that I was hearing impaired. I talked differently from the other kids, which is common when a child is hard of hearing.

My parents took me to get tested and turns out I was hard of hearing in my left ear. The school had a system in place for kids like me. I had daily speech therapy classes, where I learned how to speak and practice words. I was given a headset to wear and was told to carry it with me at all times. The teacher would wear a microphone and talk into it. This way I was able to hear her through my headset. The other kids in my class would point and laugh at me. This hurt my feelings and from there I was isolated from everyone else.

Kindergarten got better, my teacher got a class pet which was a bunny named Pearl. That bunny became my best friend. Recess was a time where we were allowed to go outside and play on the playground. Most kids in my class would look forward to this time, but not me. I would sit on the ground, eat my snack alone, and watch the other kids play.

I was eating my snack alone when a boy came up to me and asked to sit with me. I said okay, his name was Sam. He was my first best friend. We would hang out all the time, he was even in my class. Every time he made a new friend he would introduce me. My friend group began to grow. I was no longer alone.

I thought I had a friend for life. But after a couple years my first and best friend moved away. It felt awful.

From a very young age I made a key connection and decision that *I was different, and people don't like different.* I never felt that I fit in with everyone else. A key decision is a decision you make in a time of stress. You associate pain with this memory and a belief.

When you experience hearing loss, it is normal and almost expected that you speak differently. I would hear things at a different pitch and frequency. I as cautioned not to play on the road because I couldn't directionally hear oncoming cars. When my teacher would speak to me it was hard for me to understand; so for the next few years I remained in my speech therapy classes.

In speech therapy I met a new friend. Well someone who I thought was my friend. Stacy was also in resource with me. I felt more comfortable going to school knowing I had someone to hang out with and talk to.

Every year our school had a sports day. During this day we got put into teams and played different games and events. I was on a team called the lions, and our team color was yellow. There were these girls in my class that would make fun of me because of what I was wearing. I felt sad and did not understand. Even my new friend that I made joined in with these girls. I asked myself a question, why do people keep hurting my feelings? What did I ever do to them? I was so confused; I felt alone and isolated.

I had to forgive Stacy for what she did; I had no choice. My mom and her mom were friends and my mom would drop my sister and I off at her house. Every time my mom would drop us off, I began to feel deep dread and sadness. Stacy never shared her toys, she was really bossy and mean. She was a bully and did not include me in playing or talking. She liked playing with my sister more than me. I had to make the best of it because my mom had to work. I did my best not to let it affect me, but some days were harder than others. I would breakdown and cry, Stacy's mom would see me and get upset with her daughter. This did not stop her. If anything, she became increasingly awful towards me. When it was snack time she would take my snack and did not allow me to eat. She told me since it is her house and her food she gets to decide who eats it.

At school Stacy loved to push me and grab my hair. She took my school books and binders and threw them in the garbage, she would walk up behind me and push me while telling me to walk faster or she would push me into the wall.

I began to wonder why does she choose me? How come she is kind to my sister and not me? I questioned myself and wondered why this is happening to me. Anyone who has ever been bullied before asks themselves similar questions daily. It is not a quality question so I never found a quality answer. I began to pick myself apart. I thought I must not be good enough.

I wish I had the wisdom at the time to understand the deeper meaning behind what was happening. I wasn't aware that Stacy was having family troubles. When a person bullies you, it is because they don't love themselves. They have insecurities and they don't feel important in their own lives. I remember getting told not to take what others say too personally. This is hard for anyone to do. We all want to be accepted by others. We take what others say into consideration or right to heart. This is simply because we are human and as humans we feel deeply. We all have a strong need to connect with others and that connection provides a sense of safety.

CHAPTER 2

Conflict

FRIENDS ARE PEOPLE WHO we can lean on and trust. I always wanted to believe this was true. Unfortunately for me this was not true. I came to terms that it was not my path to have solid friends in my life. It was not until later in my years that I was able to trust others. I was meant to go through some harsh events in order to grow. That is how life works, we may have one unpleasant thing happen after another until the lesson or purpose is fulfilled.

Birthday parties are a big deal when you are in middle school. I got invited to my first birthday party around Halloween. We were all jumping on the trampoline when one of the girls asked me what I wanted to be for Halloween. I replied saying a devil (I had been a princess way too many times). I love the color red and already had a red dress at home. The girls began to make nasty comments. They said I am evil and they can no longer be friends with me. They ran off the trampoline and left me alone outside. I slowly walked inside the house and asked to call my mom. I sat in the driveway waiting for my mom. I could hear the girls inside laughing and having fun. I saw my mom pulling in, I ran to the car and began to cry. She asked me what was wrong. I told her nothing I just want to go home.

At school the girls from the party ignored me. They would run away and laugh anytime I was near them. I was left alone with no friends expect for my sister, who was now at the same school as me. At lunch I would hang out with her and her friends. My sister was my best friend, but she had her own friends. My sister and I are opposite. She was popular and had a bunch of friends. Then there was me, who had no friends and did not fit in. Almost every friend I did have would make fun of me. I began to feel extra nervous, get butterflies in my stomach, and feel alone.

It took me a few years before I found a new friend and was able to wean off my sisters help. My new friend Haylee and I had similar interests. We loved to make homemade videos and we both loved animals. We both were stick to one friend kind of people. This is why we worked out as friends, we would hang out all the time. We were the best of friends. Towards the end of the year, my best friend who I had known since birth was coming to the school. I was super excited and could not wait to show her around and hang out with her. Haylee was not so excited about this. When I told her about my friend Taylor, Haylee got really weird about it. She got jealous and began to spread rumors around the school about me. My trust was betrayed, the things I told Haylee in confidence were now out for others to know. I felt bare and vulnerable. Haylee stopped hanging out with me and was no longer my friend.

Outside of school I was in dance classes. I took Hip Hop and break dancing. I loved dancing. I danced with my sister since I was 4 years old. There was this girl named Maggie in my dance class who also went to my school. She was pretty close with my sister but not so much myself. My parents and her parents are friends. We would hang out and carpool to dance. I never felt like Maggie liked me. She would give me nasty looks and roll her eyes at me, she would walk by me and push me, she would ignore me when I talked to her, and she would say things to other people in our dance class about me.

I loved dance class before Maggie came along, it was a place for me where I could escape the school drama. I could get lost in music and rhythm. Because of Maggie, dance was no longer my escape, it was just like school for me. I forced myself to stay focused and ignore Maggie. I would ask my teacher to be put on the other side of the room from her. I continued to go to dance class and put on a fake smile. I remember hearing something about fake it till you make it. That is exactly what I did.

Maggie became friends with Haylee and they both began to bully me at school. They would talk about me behind my back. Write me letters with harsh words on them. Take my homework, push me in the hall. This was just the start of it for me. I always did my best to mind my own business. I never engaged with what the girls said to me at school or what they did to me.

My friend Taylor was the one person I felt safe with. She was a year younger than me, so we did not have any classes together. Taylor was the best friend that anyone could have ever asked for. One time I was in class being bullied, and I ran out of my classroom without telling the teacher. I ran directly down the hall to Taylors class and knocked on the door. Taylor was taking a test, she looked up and saw me. She got up and handed in her test even though she was not finished. She walked out of class to help calm me down. To this day I still remember this.

As the years went on the bullying continued and became more aggressive. Haylee and Maggie never stopped, they made new friends who joined in on the bullying. They would follow me into the bathroom and push me into the wall, lock me in the bathroom stall or take my backpack and throw it into the garbage. I would get threats from the girls if I ever told anyone. After school while I waited for my mom to pick me up they would bully me verbally.

My emotions got to the point where I believed the girls and what they told me. I remember my first suicidal thought was around Christmas. I remember being at a life event and suicide got brought up. The person speaking asked if anyone felt suicidal to stand up. The voice inside me told me to stand up, I was only 11. School never taught me or even talked about mental health. I had no knowledge of it. I had to drop out of dance. I did not know at the time, but I had high anxiety. I was unable to focus, as the years went on I had panic attacks and would pass out. Dance was no longer a safe place or a place where I could escape.

Years went by and my grades in school dropped. I found it hard to focus especially if the bullies were in my class. My parents were concerned but I never told them what was going on. The voice inside my head grew and haunted me.

It was my mom's birthday and she went out with her friends. My mom was friends with the parents of the bullies. Once I got home from school I went up to my bedroom to do homework. Haylee messaged me and wanted to skype and work on homework together. I was a nice person and agreed. She texted me and told me to log on. I opened up my lap top and logged on. The conversation started off normally. Then out of nowhere more girls were added to the chat. They all began to bully me. Calling me names and telling me all these awful things.

I was crushed and angry. I slammed my lap top on my bed and fell to the floor. I began to cry and scream. My sisters and dad were home. My dad ran up to my bedroom blasted open the door. Saw me on the floor and asked what was wrong. My sister ran in the door shortly after he did. My body was curled up in a ball on the floor. I was crying so hard that I was un able to speak or breathe. My entire body was shaking.

I cried for hours before I was able to calm down and speak. I told my dad and sister what happened and what was going on at school. I grabbed my lap top and logged on. When I went to the conversation the girls edited it so there was no proof. I knew they would deny everything. My dad gave me a hug and told me it was going to be okay.

My dad told me to call my mom. I called her cell phone and I began to cry again as I told her what was going on. What I did not know was that my mom was driving, and she

put me on speaker phone. Some of the girl's moms were in the car and heard everything. Once my mom got home she gave me a big hug. One of the girls who was a part of the online attack called my house and asked to speak to me. Her mom made her call me to apologize. My parents politely told her now was not a good time. It was a nice gesture that at least one of the girls made an effort to say sorry.

I went to school the next day and the bullying continued. The girl who called to apologize stopped hanging with the girls and she stopped bullying me.

I got more threats from the girls. My parents reached out to some of the girl's parents to tell them what was going on. The parents did nothing, they denied it and protected their child. My mom stopped being friends with these people.

Since I was barely passing school my science teacher called in my parents. I had to sit there and listen to her tell my mom I would never pass her class and that I didn't belong at this school. She continued to say, I should go to a school for kids with learning disabilities and that would be a better fit. My mom tried to come up with a solution such as hiring a tutor for the next 2 weeks of spring break, so I could grasp the concepts of chemistry better. I could be tested once spring break was over to see if I could move on with the rest of the class in earth science. The teacher was adamant that I would never pass. This was crushing to hear. My inner voice was agreeing with her that I wasn't good enough. I would never be good enough and I should just leave school. She didn't want me a part of her class; I knew this already because she would give me a disappointing look and send me to the resource center. The whole situation outraged my parents. My parents told my principal what happened along with the bullying. He told my parents not to worry and that he would get on it right away.

His idea of taking care of it was having the school counselor set up an ambush. The counselor pulled me aside and took me to her office. I walked through her door and saw the girls who bullied me. I was so terrified that my body froze, I was unable to speak or move. Once the meeting ended I ran out of her office. I ran right out of the front door of the school. I could hear teachers yelling at me to come back. I did not care, I ran as fast as my legs could take me. I went all the way home.

The next day at school the counselor thought it would be a good idea to have the girls who were in my classes sit outside in the hallway and put me by the door. This was so useless and stupid if you ask me. I did not feel safe at all. At this point both myself, and my parents were fed up with the school. Clearly, they were only making matters worse

and were not helping. Since I was also getting bullied online which happened outside of school; my principal said he could not do anything. School is supposed to be a safe place. They are supposed to keep an eye out for their students. Their job is to keep me safe. Instead my teachers would see and watch me get bullied and do nothing, simply turn their heads. It was hurtful and degrading.

This is when my parents pulled me from school and I left. I did the rest of my school year online. Even though I was not in school the girls still continued to bully me. They would message me on social media, make fake accounts using my name, they would even post photos of me and write things on them.

During this time. I developed many mental health issues which I was not aware of. I always felt as there was something wrong with me. My mind never shut off. I had compulsive thoughts which changed by the second. School is a place where we grow and find ourselves. I lost myself to the war of inner self. I had trouble breathing and thinking. I felt numb a lot of the times. I felt overwhelming amounts of pain.

I had eczema all over my face and neck since my body was in fight or flight mode all the time. My eczema was so bad that my eyes and lips would swell up to the point where I was unable to see or open my mouth. My health was really declining. I even had a bad case of mono that caused me bedridden for weeks sick and exhausted.

My anxiety was so high that I was unable to go out with my parents for dinner. My sister was not allowed to have her friends over at the house, since girls were a trigger for my anxiety and I would black out and seizure. It was common to have 6 panic attacks daily. This would consist of me falling and often hitting my head. The last thing my brain needed was more traumas. After having an episode during dance class I had to drop out of dance too.

My depression was so low that I was unable to communicate and be around my family. My social life became non-existent. I was falling behind in schoolwork since I couldn't focus. I did not get a single minute or hour of sleep, this was from my PTSD. I was terrified to be left alone. I would have flash backs daily of incidents where I got bullied. It was a constant repeat when I finally came back to the present I would black out or yell and scream. Every day and night I was in extreme amounts of pain, mentally and physically. I looked awful and I felt awful. I had bad acne from all the stress and impressive black circles under my eyes from lack of sleep. I began to cut and burn myself as a way for me to feel less, to disconnect and check out.

This became an addiction. I could only wear long sleeve shirts and pants for so long. When my parents found out, they took me to the doctors, and then to counselling. The thing about going to counselling was I would leave feeling even worse than before. I never felt as they understood me, all they were doing was pushing things on me. At the end of my session I still had my demons following me, still had the PTSD, anxiety, and depression. My mom had to hide all of the medication, knives and sharp objects in my house. I lost my way. I was numb. I told myself there is no point in living, nobody liked me, the girls at school told me I should die anyways, I got told I was useless, ugly, a whore, worthless and many other things. I wanted to end the overwhelming amounts of pain.

This is where I began attempting suicide. It got so bad that I had to be on 24-hour watch and monitoring since I would keep attempting to take my life. I did not want to be on earth, I did not want to finish high school. I did not care about anything. I had given up all hope, I had given up breathing and living. I began to write in a journal. This was a way for me to express my feelings without talking to someone. I got this wrap around bracelet which said hope. I wore the bracelet every day. The word *Hope* to me stood for "hold on pain ends". I really wanted to believe this, I already had used up a lot of my will power.

The moment that changed everything for me was my younger sister. It was her sweet 16 birthday coming up. I built up the courage to go to the mall and go shopping. I bought her a heart ring as memory of me and my love. I wrapped up her present and wrote her two notes. One note was wishing her happy birthday and how proud I am of her. The next note was my explanation note. I explained to her in the note that she could not have done anything to prevent me from leaving. I told her I was at peace and out of pain and that I loved her. I had a plan to take my life a couple months before her birthday.

I followed through with my plan and this is what changed my life. I blacked out and had an out of body experience. I got shown all the people who would be affected by my passing. I was shocked, I did not think anyone cared about me. I believed I was invisible to people. I realized in this moment how selfish my thoughts and actions had been. I decided to stay on earth and find the strength within myself. I wanted to be able to make a better life for myself. I wanted to be alive and feel alive. I wanted to be a positive role model for my sister. I had to be alive to look out for her and look after my dog. I once had so much anger and stress that I could not see a way through it. I lost all hope and had given up.

At my lowest moment is when I found the strength inside me. I found the strength to carry on, the strength to create a better life for myself. A life that I wanted to live. I made the decision that I was no longer going to be a victim. I knew if I wanted something different in my life I had to "DO" something different in my life. I had to change everything, and I did.

Once I decided to make a change in my life, things got better. I let go and got rid of a lot of anger and stress. My face cleared up, I found the strength to stop cutting. I got my panic attacks and depression under control. I did miss a lot of school due to my health issues, but I was able to catch up. I learned how to love and accept myself.

There are many things I actively did to heal. I journaled, I went for long runs, I spent time with my dog, I let people in my life again, I noticed all the things that were great instead of dwelling on what wasn't great. I empowered myself with meditation and yoga, I studied psychology and spent a lot of time researching and understanding anxiety and depression. I stopped self-sabotaging myself if I had a bad day. I took it one day at a time and had faith I was moving towards wellness. I closed the chapter of suffering and happiness followed.

Looking back on my life. I never gave up, I kept fighting. In our darkest moments is when we find the courage and strength that we never knew we had. Next time you find yourself in a dark place or moment remember that you are a survivor and keep fighting. It might be one hour or one day at a time but know even the smallest progress is still progress. Life never stays still or stagnant, it changes and moves forward and so will you. You will get through it.

There are many ways that you can go about telling someone if you are struggling. You can write an email or letter to your parents if you do not feel like talking to your parents, you can contact a local health line, or research mental health and the different types of disorders. We all have strength and courage within us. Realizing we need help is the first step. Second step is telling someone. Things will get better everything is temporary. We are all on a powerful soul journey. Our path is not always green grass and pretty flowers.

CHAPTER 3

Safety

SCHOOL WAS NOT ALL bad. I did have one positive aspect for me. This was my guy friends. I can honestly say they all played a huge role in saving my life. They were so much more to me then my best friends. They were my safe place, my escape and space to be free, my protectors. Because of them I had a reason to wake up every morning. I had the motivation to go to school.

The first guy friend I ever made was in grade 8. I went to my school to see what classes I got for the year. Here I was introduced to my first best friend. Little did I know he would change my life forever. School became a brighter place for me. We would sit together in class, hang out at lunch and after school. He and I both lived very close to each other.

Our friendship grew and everyday got stronger. I found out he got bullied at school too, just like me. The kids at school did not like us but this was one of the many things we had in common.

I opened up and told him about what was going on at school. He was the first person I ever told. He already knew since he would witness the bullying.

Every morning before school he would get to school early to greet me or meet me and walk with me to school. He would walk with me to my locker, my class, and walk me home. Him and I were joined at the hip. We were so close that strangers would tell us we looked like brother and sister. After that comment we began to call each other just that. He was someone I could depend on. I would text him at 4 am and tell him about how I could not sleep or if I was upset. He would come to my rescue no matter what time it was.

He was my rock and one of the many reasons why I am still here today. In the darkest moments of my life he was the light. My flashlight in the darkness holding my hand. This one time I ran out of the school counsellor's office balling my eyes out. He was walking down the hall and I bumped into him. I looked up and saw it was him. I fell down into his arms. He wrapped his arms around me and held me. There we were in the middle of the school hallway, with people

walking by. He picked me up and took me outside to talk. I told him how I could not continue the school day. He told me it was okay. He grabbed my things and walked me home.

The following year I made more guy friends. I got to be a part of this group which I looked up to for years. We would all hang out before and after school along with at lunch. Over the years the group changed and drifted. People were leaving and coming into the group. Eventually there were not many of us left.

When this happened, we became really close with one another. Every weekend we would hang out and do fun things. Such as go karting, laser tag, video game night, movie night, swimming, game night, or we would chill at my place. Every weekend I would look forward to this.

The good times and memories with the guys kept me alive and gave me hope. Not all of them knew what was going on with me. There was only two people in the group who knew. I had some of my guy friends in my classroom which was nice because I had protection. Lunch time, which once used to be a terrifying vulnerable time for me. Now was my safe place. A time and place where I was surrounded by my guy friends. Their laughter, jokes, and constant hugs embraced me with kindness and it kept me afloat. Even when I got pulled from school they kept in contact with me.

I am forever grateful for the friendship I was able to have with each one of them. The girls who bullied me could not touch me or bother me as long as I was with my group.

My last year of high school my parents asked me to go back to public school. I found a new school and I agreed to go. The thing about going to a new school in your last year is, everyone already had their friend groups and had known each other since middle school. I did not mind being an outsider since I was used to it. Within the first month of school I had an encounter with some mean girls. I ended up getting a black eye and a concussion in gym glass. I wanted to believe it was an accident but the school called my parents and said they were doing an investigation. After interviewing witnesses it appeared it was not an accident. I was pulled from school and continued to do school online.

Second semester of school I went back. I still had a lot of anxiety and struggled with depression. My parents set up appointments for me to see my school counselor daily. This helped me a lot. She was such a kind soul, she understood me and listened to my needs. She became a friend to me. I trusted her, and her office was a safe place. She went out of her way to make sure I was taken care of physically and emotionally. She found me an animal rehab center where I volunteered at and got school credit (I had a huge love for animals), she helped me be a part of this group in school which helped with bullying, she suggested joining the school play which is where I made some friends, she suggested some friends who are really kind people, and she even made it so I was able to leave each of my classrooms early to get to my next class. This way I would not be overwhelmed by all the people in the hallways. Even now that I am out of school she still checks in. She helped me through some of the hardest times and moments in my life.

To every negative there is always a positive. Even though school was a scary place for me and I experienced a lot of negative things. I also got to experience some positive and make the best of my life. We all go through things in life. We can choose to focus on all the bad things that happened to us, or we can change our perspective and find the lessons in each experience.

CHAPTER 4

Companionship

IT IS VERY TRUE that dogs are a human's best friend. My dog Sadie was born September 16, 2007. Sadie was brought into my life December 19, 2007. I truly believe that Sadie is an angel sent to me. She played a really big role in keeping me alive.

My dog Sadie was by my side through all my ups and down. She was very in tune with my emotions. When I was upset she would come up to me and sit on my lap. Every time I cried she would kiss my tears away. She would snuggle me every night, through all my sleepless nights and nightmares she was there.

I was paranoid to leave my house. I was always on alert, and I was ready to go into fight or flight mode at any moment. With my dog I felt safe, the only way I would leave my house was with my dog. Sadie was small enough to fit in any purse I had. Eventually Sadie became my service dog and not a purse dog.

I believe dogs are here to help us and teach us how to love deeper than we ever thought we could. They also teach us to be happy and to forgive. Sadie taught me how to laugh again, to be happy, to trust, and enjoy the little things. Sadie truly is a gift. I always wanted a dog from a very young age. Every single day I would ask my mom for a dog. My mom gave in and ended up getting me one. The rule was that I had to take care of all her needs. When my mom first found Sadie, she was already sold. My mom was very upset, she felt it in her gut that Sadie was meant to be ours. She continued to look for a dog.

My mom received a call, the people who were going to buy Sadie did not want her. My mom was super happy. Sadie was in Smithers, so she had to go on an airplane. I will always remember going to the airport to pick her up. Holding her little tiny white fluffy body in my arms. The way that Sadie was brought into my life was true guidance and bliss.

I truly believe that dogs are sent to us from above. Dogs are angels and are here to help guide us and to protect us. They embody true joy, loyalty and the traits of a good friend. A dog always knows how to change your state, just by showing up with their playful and loving nature.

Having a dog inspired me to want to help other dogs that were in need. One day I was watching a commercial on TV that nearly broke my heart. I am sure you seen it. You want to rip your eyes away from the screen because it is so painful to watch all these dogs suffering from abuse, but you can't. The song playing in the background was, "In the arms of an angel" by Sarah McLachlan and if you weren't crying you must have a heart of stone. I had a hard time erasing that commercial from my memory. I became somewhat obsessed about finding ways I could earn money to donate to this worthy cause. I was only 11 years old but I made up flyers and put them all over the dog parks, I handed out business cards and I started a dog sitting business. All my earnings and my allowance I donated to the local SPCA. I remember bringing in baggies of heavy change and crumbled up bills to the counter at the SPCA. My parents later told me that they saw a big shift in me when I took this on because they could see I wasn't doing well in school and they were worried. They said school was a struggle but helping dogs was a place I could win at. I thought about this. Not everyone

will naturally find school easy; therefore it is important to look outside of school for your win. I expanded my learning for dogs and found a dog trainer who mentored me and taught me everything he knew. He didn't charge me, he was happy to help. I am forever grateful for his generous and kind heart. I also got my veterinarian assistant certification when I was 14. Don't let your age stop you. If you are sincere and passionate people want to help you.

CHAPTER 5

Power of Fear

I HAVE TO TALK about fear because it is the one emotion that feeds anxiety. We all have things we are fearful of. Fear is a powerful word, a lot of us attach emotion or even memories to this word. I latched on to a certain moment in my life where I experienced a lot of fear. I allowed this moment to have power over me.

I Had a lot of surgeries in my life, this was partly because of my hearing. The first surgery I ever had went really well. It was a positive experience for me. I got to lay in bed watching the movie Free Willy. I got given a popsicle to have until I went to sleep. Six months later I had to have another surgery.

The ear tubes that I got put in fell out and left a big hole, damaging my hearing even more. This surgery was not at all what I expected. I did not get to watch Tv until I got put to sleep. I was placed onto a cold metal hospital bed, and then got wheeled into the surgery room. As I looked around I saw the big white lights above my head, sharp tools and machines. I began to freak out right away. I was screaming and crying. The nurse left to grab my parents. I was not a happy camper, it did not matter what my parents told me. I was not going to allow the nurse or doctor to touch me. The doctor made the call to cancel the surgery, this meant I would have to wait another year. My parents said no we are doing this. I had one nurse hold me down, while another gave me a needle. There was another nurse putting a gas mask on me as well. My parents were beside me telling me to take deep big breaths. I began to fall asleep and as I did, I remember my parent's voices going really deep and them talking really slow.

This was a moment where I made another unconscious key decision. Doctors and nurses were going to hurt me and I needed to stay far away from them. The smell of latex gloves, the dentist office, and the doctor's office freaked me out. I would have panic attacks if my blood needed to be drawn. I allowed this moment to control my thoughts, actions, and emotions. I was unable to do simple things like get my teeth cleaned without freaking out. I realized fear was taking over me, and I needed to take back control of my life. That's the

pattern of anxiety it can often show up in new areas, that is because there is already a well known path in your brain so a new fear can jump on that well known path and create symptoms of anxiety. But I recognized what was happening so I faced my fears head on, the things that caused me anxiety I did it anyways. In the past I would never leave my house alone because I was afraid of talking to people. That day I got in my car, drove to the mall, and walked into Sephora which is a super busy store. I walked around and took some deep breaths. I proved to myself that nothing bad would happen to me. Anything that made me afraid I realized I could overcome. I had to get out of my comfort zone, so if my brain said no way, I said let's do it okay?

I broke away from fear. I became free and could live life. Once I let go of fear positivity began to flow into my life. I focused on love instead of fear. I fed love more than I fed fear. I was kinder to myself and I chose to see and give love to others. I created a new meaning for life and myself. Change your perspective on life and your whole life changes.

CHAPTER 6

Life Lessons

WHEN IT COMES TO relationships we all learn something from them. We either do the teaching or the learning. Think back to all the relationships you have had in your life. What kinds of lessons did you learn? I would imagine you gained a clear idea of what qualities you *want* in a person.

I believe all my romantic relationships taught me a lot about myself. I was able to find my voice and become clear on what I wanted. I grew as a human being in each relationship.

When it comes to our first love we learn many things. I liked a guy who told me to choose between him or my best friend. I was young and wanted to experience a relationship. I decided to say goodbye to my best friend. My best friend warned me and told me things would end badly. Things started off great, I dated this guy for almost 2 years. We had some really great memories together, we even traveled together. To other people in our school we seemed like the perfect couple. Behind the Instagram pictures and our fake smiles, there were lies. He struggled with depression which was hard on our relationship. Once he got over his battle I began mine.

I began to notice things between us were different. I began to sense something was wrong. My own boyfriend would not text or call me back. One day he called me and wanted to take me out for lunch. I expected it to be just the two of us, but he had brought a girl along with him. The whole lunch he ignored me and talked to the other girl. I stepped outside and called my mom who came and picked me up. A couple days later my boyfriend apologizes over text and wants to make it up to me. I was hanging out with my best friend at the time. I told him to come over. As soon as he got to my house he began making inappropriate side comments about my best friend right in front of us. She was so uncomfortable that she ran into my house crying.

I yelled at my boyfriend to go home as I chased inside after my best friend. I did not talk to my boyfriend for a few days. Then he showed up at my house with a Pandora bracelet as a way to make up for what he did. I was furious, as if jewelry could make up for his behaviour. At school he would ignore and hide from me. He began to treat me as if we had already broken up. I was confused and wanted answers, so I confronted him at lunch. He began to yell at me and people outside were watching us. I got up and walked away from him never looking back. I decided I had enough with him. I was struggling a lot with my own mental health. I did not need the extra stress of my boyfriend treating me badly. I later found out from one of my close friends that he was cheating on me while I was with him. He did not have the courage to break up with me, so he did everything he could to get me to break up with him. I got the clarity and peace of mind that I was looking for. Next!

My next was verbally abusive to me. He was always putting me down saying I am ugly or how what I am wearing makes me look fat. I never felt confident, how could I when I was constantly getting put down. I became really unhappy. I gained the courage to end it.

I took time to focus on myself. I wanted to get my head space and mental state back to where it should be. I wanted to be happy with life and myself. I was feeling happy and ready to find a boyfriend. Even though heartbreaks are painful, it is how life goes. We heal and do it all over again.

My next relationship started off amazing. I was really into this guy he was a year younger, but we had the same group of guy friends. We began to talk, and he got my number. We would hang out with all our friends in a group setting, along with we would hang out alone also. I was really happy and felt special with this guy. Every lunch we would hang out together, he would find me in the hall for a friendly kiss and hug before class. I was happy to have a large group of guy friends. Hanging out with them made me smile and laugh. I felt complete with my friends. My boyfriend and I would go swimming and work out together. I would watch his sport games after school, and we could talk forever and never run out of things to talk about.

I was happy. I went on Facebook one day and like most girlfriends do, I checked out his profile. I was in shock as to what I saw and found. I took pictures and kept scrolling down. He was flirting, sending hearts, and tagging a girl in relationship quotes. A girl who should have been me was not me. My heart shattered all over again. I called his best friend who was also my best friend. His best friend told me that the girl and him had history together and was not surprised if he was cheating on me. I confronted my boyfriend who had nothing to say, except that we were done. I was left heartbroken, angry and confused crying on my bedroom floor.

The word got around at school that I was single. The guy who verbally abused me found out. He would follow me to my classes, show up at my locker. He would say things along with touch me. I felt so uncomfortable and my anxiety went through the roof. I felt ashamed and never talk to anyone about it. There was another guy who went to the same school as me who was also sexually assaulting me. I had no escape, no one to protect me. I never told my parents or anyone. I felt ashamed of myself and was in disbelief of what was happening. I found myself checking out into my own world. I actually decided at that point to take night school and finishing up my grad credits online.

I got a new boyfriend who treated me as I should be treated. Our relationship was great. Until we both got out of school, we both had different views on life. Our relationship changed a lot. We were never on the same page when it came to growing and achieving new things. It seemed as one of us was always behind and trying to catch up. The feeling of insecurity set in which caused a lot of fights. Which lead to laziness and the feeling of hopelessness. One of us was always holding back their greatness to be on the same page.

I had a fear of being alone and so did he. We held on to each other when we should have said goodbye. We began to fight all the time. We would break up and get back together, it was a vicious cycle. Our fights became violent and we would end up hurting each other, but we stayed together. We both did not have any one else in our lives except for each other. It got to the point where the relationship took a toll on both of our mental states. I was depressed all the time, I was no longer happy. I felt trapped and lost. I made the hard choice of leaving and blocking him. I believe this was the best thing to do for both of us. It was a decision made from love.

I understand in order to attract our perfect relationship we have to get clear on what we want. Then we have to decide how we need to show up and *be* in order to attract that kind of relationship. We can't assume it is going to just fall into our laps, although sometimes we are ready and it does. It is always best to work on ourselves first so we can bring the best version of ourselves to the relationship. We can save ourselves a lot of pain if we do this. Think about your energy, your attitude, and your emotions you will bring to it. Think about what you will give, more than what you will get. A great relationship is built on giving, not getting. We want to create quality relationships so we have a quality life. Some of you may be thinking I am way too young to know this, but I am an old soul that has experienced many life times and I have been gifted with downloads of my past and current lessons so I can be a voice for good.

I like to look at life as a learning experience and an opportunity. Everything we go through has a higher and greater purpose. Do not believe everything you see because you may be looking through dirty glasses. Do not judge others as others are a reflection of ourselves. We all have ups and downs. No matter what you are going through always be kind to yourself and others. Sometimes we have to thank our adversaries, they call us to grow. If you are being challenged it is because you are trusted to it. Don't feel sorry for yourself, it is a special circumstance just for. There is always a higher learning. Be grateful and thankful for all the things you learned in your relationships. Even the not so good ones because their soul was called to be your worthy opponent and to help you learn a lesson. Sometimes we need to experience some frogs before we meet our prince (*wink, wink*). When one ends look forward to a fresh start, and a new chance. Don't beat yourself up and consider it a failure. This is no failure, only learning. In life we always have a chance to start a new chapter or a new season.

CHAPTER 7

Forgiveness

FORGIVENESS CAN BE A hard topic for a lot of us. Myself I had trouble with this one. Over time we get older and wiser. I learned that the people who hurt us need the most love. The ones who hurt others do so to feel significant. To feel better about themselves. Learning to love others and let go is the most powerful and healing thing.

I developed so much anger and hate towards the girls that bullied me. I was so caught up in the emotions of anger that I did not realize I was just like them. I was letting anger control my life. *I became a bully to myself.* I sabotaged friendships because I came up with this story that all girls are bad and will hurt me. The one thing that I wanted most, which were friends; I told myself I could not have because I am not good enough along with I did not want to get hurt. In the end I was hurting myself.

When it came to relationships I had a bad mindset going into them. I had the fear of getting cheated on or not being good enough. Since I was always thinking this, it ended up happening. That is the thing with our minds they are very powerful. The things that we focus on we also put energy into. We end up making our thoughts true whether we are aware of it or not. Our thoughts create our reality.

How can we forgive ourselves or forgive someone? How do we move on and move past the hurt? It is up to yourself to want to move passed the hurt, anger, guilt, and sadness. Whatever emotions you may be feeling you can change it. A lot of the times we hold onto those emotions because we are getting attention from others. You may not want to let go of the feeling of guilt, hurt, or anger because other people give you sympathy. We create an addiction to our problems because it meets our needs. We may lack connection with people but we have a big connection to our problems. If you find you are absorbed in your problems get out in the world and help others with theirs. It is a great way to break the pattern and you are filling your needs in a more empowering way by helping someone else. Ask yourself by holding onto these emotions do you benefit in a positive or negative way?

The emotion of love is the strongest and most powerful of emotions. For a lot of us we live our life by one focused emotion which drives us. I switched from anger to compassion. I realized people are innocent at their core and that their behaviour may be bad but their soul good. Hurt people; hurt people. They are running a temporary program until they learn better. Everyone is learning that is why we are having a human experience. They were doing their best with what they know at the time. We all grow up in different homes, role models and backgrounds. Not one of us are the same. We all view life differently. I accepted them and myself for who I am. Once you accept what has happened to you, change begins to happen. I sent love to myself, and to those who hurt me. Instead of judging what happened, I looked at it from a different perspective. All the people who have come into my life have been a blessing. My life has changed and been impacted because of everyone who has entered my life.

Without the girls who bullied me I would not be passionate about mental health. I would not be on the path to help change people's lives. Without my school teachers I would never have done online school and then gone to a new school. The new school which had amazing teachers who cared. My school counsellor became my friend and advocate. She was there for me when I needed her the most

or when I simply just wanted to talk. She was the one who pushed me when I was lost in the dark. She celebrated my achievements and progress with me. The relationships I had taught me a lot about myself along with the qualities I want in a forever person.

Once you forgive, you begin to live your life in a new perspective. You have a new outlook on life, a new you. The next chapter of your life begins. Be free and live your life the way you deserve. Every day is a chance to start over. A chance to better the person you were yesterday. Let your soul be free.

CHAPTER 8

Signs Before The Gifts

I HAD A LOT of weird things happen to me in my life that I did not understand or was unable to comprehend.

When I was 15 years old I attempted to take my life. I felt myself moving backwards as if I was on the wrong track and being sucked up in a vacuum. I went up to this super blinding bright white place. I could not see much except white light. I heard a man's voice, it was very deep. The voice said my name. I felt some weird sort of comfort knowing that this person knew my name. At the same time, I was still very confused as to where I was. The voice spoke again telling me welcome. He began to tell me that he has been watching me. I thought to myself well this is creepy. He began to tell me I was welcome to come home and stay or go back. Although

I had no idea where I was I felt an overwhelming sense of love and peace.

He told me if I choose to go back, life would become harder for me. My strength and ability to pull myself out of darkness would be tested. As an end result if I passed all of the tests I would receive a gift on my 20th birthday. If I stayed in this white light place, I would be reunited with friends, family, and animals. I would get to stay in a place of love, light, peace, and no judgement. The pain I was experiencing would be gone forever. I thought about staying in this strange but oddly familiar place. I then began to think, "Who would look after my dog and sister? Who would protect them?" I then decided I wanted to stay and fight, I knew it was not going to be easy. Let me tell you it was not easy. Life tested me in all areas of life.

One year later when I was 16. I woke up and there was a sparkly diamond brooch beside my bed side table. I asked my family members and they never seen it before. Later during the year my mom took me to a yoga class. I was dealing with extreme anxiety and panic attacks. My mom thought yoga would be a good idea. It was my first time trying yoga. The class was a lot of movement and stretches, towards the end of class we did a closed eye process where we sat in the silence.

I went into a meditative state. I felt myself floating, next thing I knew I was in this strange place again. I heard the same voice as last time. A deep loving voice of a man. I was so frightened that I could not move. This time there was another person, a man with dark skin standing beside this other man.

The dark skin man had a presence that made me feel safe and warm, as I could trust him. This man was smiling at me but did not speak, he held out a hand to me. The other man told me everything is okay and to take his hand. I was led to this room where a movie began to play. It was a movie about me, I was getting shown images and scenes of my life. When the movie was done playing I understood my life, my purpose, and the reason why things happened to me. Everything happened for a reason and a purpose, one thing led to another in my life. The man who I met before looked at me and spoke to me. He thanked me for being strong throughout all of the tests. I was told someone special was going to come into my life, and they would be a gift from him. When I came back to the present I began to cry uncontrollably. Thankfully the yoga class was finished, and we could leave. I was unable to explain what happened until I got home. My mom was amazed, and she believed what I was telling her even though I felt crazy.

When I turned 17 I was feeling as I did not belong. My anxiety was high, I was unable to go out in public alone. I was getting frustrated with myself. I continued to do the things that helped with my mental state. This was writing in my journal, making vision boards, and working out. This one day I was in the gym working out and my emotions were not the best, I was feeling overall really down and anxious.

During my workout I heard a loud ringing noise in my ears, this made me stop. I then heard bells chiming. Something told me to look up, as I did angel wings fell from the sky. The angel wings landed right in front of me. I looked around to see if anyone else had just seen what happened. I reached down to pick up the wings, as I did the ringing and bell chime stopped. The wings were sliver and had a loop at the top. I kept the wings with me and went to the mall to find a chain, so I could wear the wings as a necklace.

A few months later, I was sleeping and woke up to a man's voice saying my name. I could not see anything. The voice spoke and told me the hard part was over. All of the tests I went through were to prepare me for what was about to happen next. The voice told me to be patient, to listen, and watch for the signs. The next morning when I woke up, one of my dad's friends reached out to me and invited me to go on a trip and be his guest. It was a very last-minute trip. I

was searching for answers as to why my emotions were so high all the time. I felt as going away would be a nice break from reality and I would find some answers.

Just before I left for my trip to lake Tahoe my dad called. He began to tell me he met a medium and had a session. The medium told my dad that one of his daughters had super natural abilities. My sister and I laughed and thought my dad totally got scammed of his money. My mom suggested to me that I was the one with super natural abilities and that is why I had high anxiety. For the first time ever, I thought my mom was crazy. I did not believe in life after death. I had no faith in which I believed in. Religion was confusing and didn't make sense to me. I packed my bags and got ready for my trip.

CHAPTER 9

Courage

I LANDED IN TAHOE and got in an Uber. The ride from the airport to the hotel was 2 hours. While I was in the Uber, I began to pick up weird things and have weird thoughts. I saw an image of a car crash and a young male who passed. I began to hear his voice. I wanted to ask my driver and talk about what I was seeing, to see if she knew anything about a car crash. I kept quiet since the driver might have thought I was crazy, and quite frankly, I felt crazy. The thoughts quickly went away and so did the images. I put my headphones in and stared out the window.

I arrived at the hotel. I got settled in and grabbed some food. I called my parents to let them know I arrived safely. I kept to myself and did not make an effort to talk to anyone. I am very shy in that way, I have anxiety when I am around people. I am not sure what to say or how to act. Keeping to myself was the best thing for me at this point. The place where I was staying at was very beautiful. It was a log house surrounded by trees with a view of the water.

The second day of my trip I was standing outside on the balcony. I was looking out at the ocean and trees admiring the view when I saw a short old lady standing beside me. She was 5 feet tall, had glasses, and short grey hair. She looked at me, smiled, and said, "I need you to find my grandson and talk to him." I looked at her with a confused look and walked back inside. She followed me and kept telling me to find her grandson. I ignored her, feeling confused as to why she would not leave me alone or go talk to someone else.

I walked upstairs to grab some dinner. While I was eating my food, a guy sat beside me. His Name was Kyle. He asked how I was doing. I replied, "great". I asked him how he was doing. He told me how he was feeling sad and not doing good, because his grandma past away. He was close to his grandma. Suddenly, the grandma was back beside me saying, "you found him! That is my grandson." I abruptly excused myself from the table and began to cry. I was so confused, as to what the heck was going on.

One of the ladies came up to me and helped calm me down. She told me that I was gifted. She explained to me that what I was seeing, and hearing was somewhat normal. What she said helped me accept what I was experiencing.

Later on, I was picking up strange things about my parents. I decided to call them and talk to them about the information I was picking up. It turns out that I had a brother, but he never made it. I was able to meet him on the other side and talk to him. I was feeling what my brother felt. I knew the day he was going to be born, how old he would have lived to, how his purpose was not to make it to earth. I knew the name my parents were going to give him. I could see him and talk to him as if he was a real person standing in front of me. I was able to deliver a message from him to my parents, which caused amazing amounts of healing for them. My life was also touched to have been able to meet my brother. I always wanted a brother, I felt as my life would have been different. I would have had someone to protect me. This was not the case as much as I wished it was. I was meant to learn how to fight my own battles, to use my own voice and speak up.

I walked back inside the room. I looked outside the window and there was a grizzly bear. The bear was staring right at me and was so close to the house. I yelled, "Look there's a bear!" Everyone came running over to check it out. One of the ladies told me the meaning of spotting a bear. That meaning was courage (which ironically, was exactly what I needed in that moment). My dad's friend who invited me on the trip, asked me if I would share my gift and knowledge with everyone. I was nervous and still unsure if what I was seeing, and hearing was true. I thought of the bear and the meaning. I decided to go for it.

I sat outside on the balcony with 22 people sitting around me looking at me. Waiting for me to speak. I began to tell them about the grandma I saw. I began to speak about what was happening. As I opened myself up I was able to pick up on other peoples loved ones who had passed. I was able to know things in the present and future about people who I have never met!

Everyone was shocked and so was I. I had no idea how I knew these things. I trusted myself and explained what I was seeing. I had the courage to bring healing to others and release them from their grief. I was amazed at myself and the impact I had on a stranger's life. Every single day I think back to the bear. How truly guided the whole experience was. I feel I have such a strong connection to bears. Anytime I am feeling like I cannot do something I think back to the bear.

CHAPTER 10

The Shift

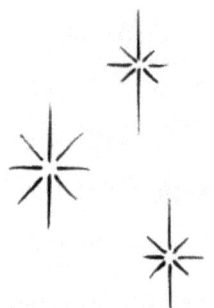

MY WHOLE LIFE TURNED upside down. Everything that I knew about myself was unknown. I had to learn who I was and learn to love myself all over again.

I got the sense of peace, and clarity I was looking for. I understood my emotions and thought process. I learned that a lot of the times my thoughts and the voices in my head were not my own. Anytime I would feel anxiety it was simply spirits from the other side coming into my space. My panic attacks were a way for my body to protect itself. I was receiving so much information from the other side that I had no way to understand it or ground myself. My body did the only thing it knew to bring me back to the present moment, and that was to pass out. It was like a re-set breaker switch.

It was hard for me to adjust. I felt like a toddler learning and seeing life for the first time. I felt more alone than ever before. I did not have anyone to talk to or help me understand what I was seeing. I reached out to a group who had similar abilities (so I thought) in hopes they would help me and be my friends. The first meeting my instinct told me to leave. I was seeing words on the ceiling. "Warning" "Unsafe" "Beware". I was being warned but from what? Why was there a light bubble of protection around me? What followed really creeped me out and I knew this was not the right group for me. This experience filled my head with fear, which caused me to become afraid of my gift.

I felt even more crazy. The voices and images got more intense. I had no control over anything. I was not able to sleep because I would have 15 people standing at my bed talking to me and I was the only one who could see this. I learnt to keep things to myself. To trust my friends on the other side. I spent a lot of time exploring the other side and talking to people. I learnt about who I am and how I work. I decided to share my gift with others. I wanted to help impact their lives along with answer any unsolved questions.

I made a website and began to tell my friends and family. Every session I did I was bang on. I shocked myself with what I knew and was able to pick up on. I kept going and kept sharing my knowledge. Oddly enough I always wanted to be a counsellor and help people with their problems. I took schooling before I ever found out I was gifted and was able to get certified as a life coach. This came in handy when dealing with people's relationships, guilt, and grief.

I never lost anyone close in my life. I had never experienced loss in my own life. I was dealing with people who lost their dog, friend, lover, or family members every day. In December 2017 I lost one of my best friends.

I woke up one morning to my best friend standing at the end of my bed. I sat up in my bed and asked him how he got in my house, if he was in trouble, and if he was okay? He stared at me with a blank expression on his face. He came close to me and sat beside my bed. He told me to take his hand and so I did.

I became his soul for a brief moment. This tends to happen to me. When I am talking to spirit they will allow me to experience how they felt. I will re live their final moments. I also get brought to the scene or taken to a place that is significant to them. At times they allow me to go into their loved one's house to point something out. I feel the emotions

and get to see life through their eyes. He began to tell me, how he was free from all the pain on earth. The judgement, confusion, and everything he was going through. He was free from it all. This transition hit me hard, I absorbed the energy when I should have released it. I was unable to leave my house for weeks. I did not want to come to terms and accept that he was gone.

I pulled myself together and remembered all of the amazing times we had together. All the year-end school parties we had thrown together, all of our laughs and jokes, every weekend spent at my house watching movies, and going out laser tagging or shopping. I remember him always checking in on me to see how I was doing or reaching out when he needed help. He was always putting others first. He saved my life when I was at my end, I wish I was able to return the favor.

I know now it was not his path to be saved. There was nothing anyone could do. He is serving a higher purpose and helping so many people from the other side. He is with me daily popping in to make jokes. To go on a car ride with me and rap along beside me. To even offer advice when I need it or make fun of my music choices. No matter where I go, I know he is with me. I appreciate all he ever did for me.

CHAPTER 11

Other Side

THE MOST COMMON AND known word for someone who has super natural abilities is a Medium. There is also a light worker, spiritual warrior, spiritual coach, and many more. I do not like to put a label on myself, in a way I am the same as you. We all have different and unique talents that set us aside from everyone else.

Sharing my knowledge and information is a healing process for both myself, and the client. I am able to connect to the other side from your energy field. We all have our own energy that we operate on, along with spirits from the other side who are with us daily. We have a guide who can be a person from a past life, current life, an animal, or a higher dimension creature. Our guide is assigned to us before we come down to earth. They have gone through a similar life path to the one we are currently on.

When I am having a session with someone, I communicate with their guide, my guide, and the higher power. I work with your energy and the energy on the other side. The information in each session will vary. Spirit is in charge of bringing up what will benefit you and your higher self. A lot of the time we focus on who and what we want to come through. This creates a forced energy. In a way we are forcing a loved one to come through. Not all spirits who have passed on wish to speak. We become caught up with thinking hard about this person or animal. This can block any other messages that need to come through. You may not relate or remember how the things I say connect to you until later.

I want to make note that the person you really want to connect with may not come through due to various reasons. They are at peace and those answers you want may not be a high agenda for spirit on the other side. I respect that, but I never force anything because my gift does not work like that. Never take it personally and don't be disappointed. Don't come up with a disempowering meaning because of it.

We all have to trust that what comes through is for the greater good. I have a great-Grandpa that pops in from time

to time and nods his head once I see him and then disappears. He never says a word. He just wants us to know he is around but doesn't want to interfere or communicate. Then I have a great-Grandma who is always communicating. Telling me I need to eat more and fatten up, filling the room with the smell of cinnamon buns, leaving dimes all over, or commenting on my day.

In order for me to channel spirit and go into depth about one's past, present, and future. The environment in which I am working in must be cleared before and after. My guide will do a full sweep removing any unwanted energy, along with protecting the space. Protecting the space in which I will be working in is important so outside spirits from other people in the house will not interfere.

When we pass on we stay the same personality wise. We still have a connection to our loved ones and are able to visit. The other side is a much higher and faster paced environment. This is where psychic abilities come forth. Everything happens on the other side before it happens down on earth. This is how I can know things before they happen. The information I get is so fast that it can be hard to pick up what spirit is saying, along with the message they want to pass along. I have learned how to slow the information down to a pace where I can understand it.

I see things, clairvoyant. I see spirit in full form with detail, very much like any other human being. I see life movie clips, I see symbols, colors, pictures, dates, numbers (license plates and addresses), and even charts of human anatomy.

I hear things, clairaudient. I can communicate telepathically with spirit and animals. I will hear songs that have a significant meaning to people. I will hear all kinds of things that are often symbolic in some way such as a bell, a dog barking, or the sound of the ocean. I have full conversations and sometimes just a few words. I also hear different languages and that is always interesting because I have to tell them I don't speak German, sorry!

I feel things, clairsentient. Sometimes I am literally taken through a life event, so I can fully understand what you went through or a passed loved one went through. Sometimes I feel strong emotions tied to various life events or circumstances. I was doing a session once and I couldn't stop coughing, I had a burning sensation in my throat, and trouble breathing. I felt like I was enveloped in smoke. I asked my client if he was caught in a burning house fire when he was very young. He had and his soul wanted to clear the trauma. It can be quite overwhelming but also extremely powerful to have that depth of understanding. This allows

me to help you move through blockages and see a clear picture of why you are running certain programs and come up with solutions. So much healing and freedom takes place when you can see the bigger picture of how your life fits together.

I just know things, claircognizant. Sometimes nothing is required to show me, tell me or feel. Sometimes I just have a strong knowing. At first, I was hesitant to share this one. But over time I learned the information was correct and all I have to do is show up with trust.

I am able to read peoples thoughts, this is called telepathy. This skill comes in handy when I am working with a client or simply with my friends and family. I have a very strong connection to animals especially to dogs. Since I was a young child my heart fell in love with every single dog out in the world. I always thought I would be a veterinarian and help save dogs, then I discovered my gift and my life went in a new direction. The cool thing about dogs is they have thoughts just like we do. They have a sub conscious mind and unconscious mind. I am able to communicate with animals through their thoughts. This comes in handy with my own dog. When I first discovered my gift, it was a strange thing being able to look at her and have a conversation without speaking.

I would say the most difficult thing for me to learn was realizing I am more than just a vessel for spirit to use. I am human, and I am in control of my life. Once I learned how to control spirit rather then they control me, I was able to feel a sense of calm and normal. When I went out in public I was seeing and receiving so much information. I wanted to help but at the same time it was very overwhelming for me. My guide taught me how to control my gift, when to shut myself down, and when to be open. There is a right time and place for being open. I still feel things and am able to pick up on things, but spirit has to respect my wishes and not come into my space.

CHAPTER 12

Past Life

WE ALL HAVE HAD a life we lived before our current one. Many, many, many past lives experiencing many forms such as female, male, animal, or plant. Everything is energy and has a consciousness. Consciousness has different levels of evolution. Depending how we passed, trauma can carry over into our current lives. This is called a soul imprint, in which our past life can imprint on our current life. When it comes to fears we may have no idea where they came from. As a child we may have had a tragic incident, which can cause us to be fearful. Most of the time it stems from our past life.

I went to a summit with my mom. She wanted me to meet more people like me. A kind, soft-spoken women approached me from her booth and explained she could tap into the soul timeline and delete effects (emotions) tied to events that don't serve our highest good. I was not sure what I was getting myself into, but my mom wanted me to try it out.

This was a very strange process but easy for me since I naturally have a connection to the other side. I would always have the same dream over and over again. Dreams are messages from the other side. Our loved ones can communicate with us through our dreams along with any past life trauma can re occur in our dreams. I would always have this dream of someone breaking into our house and kidnapping me and my sister. The kidnapper would come into our house and search for us, my sister and I would hide. Sometimes the kidnapper got us other times he did not find us. When he got us, we would be in the back of a van. I would have to kill the driver and drive my sister and I to safety.

When I was uncovering memories from a past life, I found out in one of my past lives that a similar event occurred. My sister and I went to the market with our parents. My father took my sister away from me and my mother, and then ended up selling my sister for money. My father came back and told us he lost my sister. My mother and I looked for my sister for weeks with no luck. Months went by and we never found her, but my mother never stopped looking. The money my father got from selling my sister, he used to buy us a new house. My mother was never the same, she was checked out. All she did was cry and resent me. I felt as I failed my mother and sister. It was my job to protect my sister since I was older. This is where my dream of getting kidnapped and having to protect my sister came from. I was able to realise this and create a new meaning. I moved on to another past life.

I was a man in one of my past lives. I was out on a boat with my best friend, in the middle of the ocean. We were on our way to a new island in which I discovered. My best friend pulled out a knife, stabbed me in the back, and pushed me into the water. I drowned in the ocean and passed away. In my current life I have a terrible fear of swimming in water. When it came to friends in my current life I would get stabbed in the back a lot in a metaphorical way. My soul was repeating the past. This was because my soul was not ready to let go.

My next life was a strange one. I was a male again walking in the middle of a dessert. A green goblin came up from behind me. It attacked me and then became a part of me (I know how strange this sounds). The lady doing the brain accessing of my past life began to say a prayer and talk to the creature who was then sent away. After accessing this memory, she decided to stop because we were way over an hour. When I came back to the present moment she handed me a piece of paper, she told me to read it. Of course, I never did read it. I went home and went straight to bed, exhausted.

I woke up in the middle of the night with the worse stomach ache and body pain. I began to throw up every hour on the hour. This went on throughout the whole night, I developed a high fever. I had to work the next morning along with the following day. I decided to find the piece of paper the lady who worked on me had wrote. I saw on the back near the bottom. "You May experience a 48-hour fatigue and defragging stage." This gave me some piece of mind as to what I was experiencing was normal, but it still did not make matters any better. Throwing up was a way for my body to release any unwanted energy and get things out of my system. My body was finally getting rid of the energetic attachments and this threw me into a whole new level of healing. Every time I would throw up I thanked my body, even though it was a painful process. I decided to come from love and gratitude. This was happening for me, not to me.

CHAPTER 13

Soul Connections

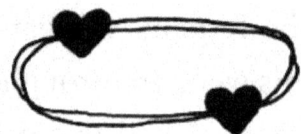

BEFORE I EXPERIENCED THE past life memories connection. I had a vision. I was in my office listening to piano music when my soul made a connection to a past life. I was sitting in my office chair one moment and the next I was on stage playing piano in front of thousands of people. I looked around. There was a red curtain beside me, I had on a shiny headband, and a black long dress with gloves. Once I finished everyone stood up and cheered. I walked off stage and someone said my name Clara Schumann.

I was back in my office chair. I thought to myself well that was strange. I have always loved classic piano music, along with I always wanted to learn how to play. I called forth my guide. He began to explain the vision I had was indeed me in another life time. I googled the name and saw the shiny head piece. The strange thing is she looks like me. Same face shape, same eye colour, same nose. I found out she became a famous piano player at a very young age. She had a husband and son who both struggled with mental health, specifically depression. In this era of time, people who experienced mental health got locked up and were given barbaric shock treatment. I did not try to help my son or husband, for I did not understand or know how to help them. In my present life I had to experience mental health, so I could better understand and empathize with my past family. It is true what they say about life coming full circle.

Our souls are smart but also sensitive. When we are out and about we can pick up other emotions. This is because some of us are more sensitive than others. We may also meet someone and have an instant connection. We may feel as we have known this person for years even though we just met. Our souls recognize another soul in a human body. This is where love at first sight comes from, along with the feeling of knowing someone. In a life before this one, you had a life with that person you feel a connection to. I never thought I would experience love at first sight, until I did.

I am not one who goes out and socializes with people. I am very much so a home body. I love to be at home and hang out alone in my room. It was one of my friend's birthday and

he was throwing a party. My friend lived 4 hours away and it was winter. I told him I was not going to come. The universe ending up working in my favor. I got a last-minute work call which was in the same town as my friend. I called him and told him I would be able to make it to his party after all.

I met up with my friend beforehand, so I could get a ride to dinner. After waiting a while, his friends all walked in. I watched as this one guy walked passed me and we all went to our table. I was stunned as to how amazing and familiar his energy felt. My stomach began to fill with butterflies. He instantly began to talk to me. He asked how long I was in town for, I replied until tomorrow, but it depends. It truly did depend, I could stay in town for a few more days if I had a reason to.

He told me his name and asked for mine. I was so caught up in my own world, trying to figure out how such an attractive guy was talking to me, that I forgot my own name.

I for sure thought I blew it and would have no chance with this guy. The night went on and anytime I got up to leave the table, he would leave to follow me or wait for me. We were flirting and both very into each other. Some of the guys decided to go grab a coffee. It was snowing outside. I was wearing a thick sweater and a jacket since it was winter. The guy offered me his jacket and insisted I wear it. We chatted about life and held hands, he began to tell me how pretty and beautiful I am. He told me he found me very attractive and I told him that I found him very attractive also. The night went on and I got his number. We texted the next morning and made a plan to meet up.

Things were never awkward or weird between the two of us. We both were so comfortable, and things felt so right. Even though we both lived in different cities we were never worried. Our connection was so strong and undeniable. I ended up staying longer in town and got to know him better. From the first day of meeting him he kissed me on the cheek. He was a gentleman, super sweet, and super affectionate. He showed he cared by texting, calling, and video chatting when we were apart. I went up to visit him again the week after we met. We spent 5 days together, during this time he asked me to be his girlfriend.

I was very curious as to my past lives, and if I had one with this guy. I looked into it, and indeed we did have a past life together. I was Emily and he was Patrick. We had 4 children together and passed away close together from natural causes. When I told my boyfriend about my ability to channel spirit he was very supportive. Which surprised me but also made me love him more. His family were big believers in "the other side". He grew up learning new things

and watching tv shows about spirit. He never made me feel like I was crazy or different. He treats me with respect and appreciates the abilities I have.

Overall life works in mysterious ways. When it comes to meeting someone or seeing someone. Our souls will recognize and make a connection right away. We are just in a different human body, but our souls still stay the same. Our souls get altered and our memories from that life time get locked away. Trust yourself and the feelings you get.

CHAPTER 14

Trusting Yourself

TRUSTING YOURSELF IS A struggle for a lot of us. For me it was a whole new ballgame. I had to learn to not only trust myself but also trust spirit. To this day I am still trying to figure it out. When I meet someone, I have a hard time conversating. I have spirit throwing information at me, while the person is talking. Trying to keep myself present can be hard. We all have something we struggle with on a daily basis. Mine would have to be conversations with people. I find when I talk to people I feel them on a deeper level. I can see their inner struggles and feel how they're feeling.

I want to share messages from the other side, but not everyone is open to it. I myself even have trouble trusting that what I am feeling and seeing is true. I guess you can say, I don't want to be judged. In some ways I care what people think of me. Just like we all care what others think. I want to respect their privacy along with respect spirit knowledge. When it comes to receiving a message, I have to speed my energy up, along with slowing down spirit energy in order to deliver a message. While this is happening, I am connected to your energy and aware of what you are feeling.

You can see how when it comes to speaking in general, I can be a bit hesitant with what I say, along with what to say. There is a lot that goes on. I sense spirit around me all the time, but I will not trust it. Since I do not trust it, my guides will send me a sign. Thankfully they are patient with me when it comes to my learning. It truly is a learning process. There is no teacher beside your guide who can teach you. He will show me the color purple, place his hand on me and send me over whelming amounts of pure love, show me his face, or speak to me. He has also showed himself on my security cameras, and in pictures he tends to show up beside me to my right. I call him my guide because he guides me but it has been confirmed that he is actually an angel.

Trust is a game in which you must practice over and over. You do not learn to trust someone right away it takes time. Just like building a relationship with your guide. You must put in the effort to connect. You must remember your loved ones hear you, they are with you. When you need guidance or someone to listen, they have your back. I am learning that we all have a comfort zone in which we feel safe. If we stay in our bubble and never get out of our comfort zone. We will never grow or experience new things. We cannot experience change unless we ourselves change. You are doing something right if you are afraid. Fear comes when we venture outside of our comfort zone. Breakthroughs happen when we have fear but we forge forward through it.

My comfort zone is spending time and being by myself. Going out in public alone or having to talk to new people is out of my comfort zone. I am learning how to protect myself, so I do not feel what others are feeling. This way I can have a conversation and be fully present. In order to be present in every moment, I had to find things in the present to connect me. I would choose a colour and find things in the room around me, in which were that colour. I would also count to 10 and find 10 things in the room. One of my favorite is to re arrange my bedroom. This causes me to be fully present and enjoy my time on earth. When having a conversation with someone I allow my gut to guide me. If I feel as the person I am talking with is not pure, I will simply excuse myself. Spirit plays a huge role when it comes to trusting your gut. They will send us a feeling that others may call intuition, which is also true. Your gut will never steer you in the wrong direction.

CHAPTER 15

Opening Doors

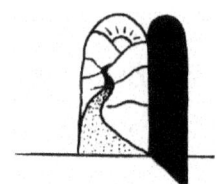

EVERY DAY WE OPEN doors in our life. Car doors, front doors, office doors. Our life moves in different directions and quite often it moves in ways we never imagined it to.

Opening a door to a new job, new relationship, or new self can most definitely be a scary thing but it does not have to be. If we do things that make us feel safe and comfortable we will never grow. We know if something scares us that in some way we will learn and grow. My gift at times can be a little scary to me. This is because it is a field that is so unknown, every session I have with someone is very different. There is a lot of uncertainty for me. I do not get to be in control of my own body or thoughts. Spirit light and wisdom takes over and controls how the session will go and what information gets brought forth. I find myself learning new skills and abilities daily.

I would not change my gift for anything. It is a learning experience for me. I get to empower and heal people who have been hurting. I allow the connection between deceased and living. I can bring peace and allow peace to happen on both sides. I can clear up any messages that spirit has been leaving for us. Whether we realize it or not there are signs all around us. Dreams that feel real can indeed be real. They can be us in another life time, or a predicament about the future. What I love doing is keeping a journal beside my bed so once I wake up I can write down my dreams. This way I can keep track of my dreams along with the message that come with my dreams. If you do not remember your dreams do not worry. We are not meant to remember the message. We may see people we do not recognize or some that we do. The people we do not recognize a lot of the times can be our guide or spirit team.

When we have a loved one who has passed over, it is very common for them to pop in our dreams. They can simply say hello, to let you know they are okay. Deliver a message such as don't go to the party, or to let you know they approve of you having their things. They can connect and say many things.

Dreams are not only a way for our loved ones to come to us. Dreams can also open up doors to our fears. Reoccurring dreams can be due to past life or a fear we have not yet faced. I remember as a child every time I had a fever, I would have the same dream. I was super tiny like a mouse, there were people and elephants all around me, and when I spoke, no one would hear me. My voice would be high pitch and fast paced. When the elephant or people would talk it would be slow and deep. I realized later in life, this dream was because I never felt like I had a voice. Any time I would speak up to the girls who bullied me, they would not hear me or stop. I felt useless and defenceless. This dream would always scare the crap out of me, as I got older I used my voice. The dream stopped, and I never had it again.

CHAPTER 16

Balance

WHEN IT COMES TO life it is easy for us to worry about problems we *may* have in the future. Change and growth happen in the present and we can't create if we are energetically stressed about the future or obsessing about the past. I drift when I am not energetically present. I would spend a lot of my time thinking and worrying about what is to come. It is common trait of anxiety and I was unconsciously not being present. I never was one with my body or grounded to earth, I had to always be mindful of this until I created a new pattern and habit of being present.

I had to learn to bring myself back to earth. To connect

and be one with myself. Having time to yourself is so important for your soul to re-charge. Being around people and taking in their energy or walking by someone can be overwhelming at times. Do something you love. Take a bath, light some candles, put on some soft lighting and music, write how you feel in a journal and what causes you to feel that way. Meditation is also great for your mind and soul. I put on some calming music and sit with my thoughts, or I will do a breathing exercise depending on how I am feeling.

Mother earth is a great source to bring balance. She provides trees for us to breathe, clean air, animals and plants, along with a beautiful nature for us to feel at peace. Calling on her to help ground and take away unwanted energy is great. I like to imagine that I am a tree and my feet are roots going deep into the earth. As you inhale picture gold or white light coming through your body. This is healing energy. Then as you exhale picture a red or grey energy leaving your body. This will help all unwanted energy to be absorbed into mother earth. I remember reading something that said, "Mother earth needs our shit in order for plants to grow." So don't feel bad giving it to her because she knows what to do with it.

You may have heard the term "empath". An empath is someone who can feel others emotions on a deep level. I

find most people with high anxiety are very strong empaths. In some way we are all empathetic. No matter where we go there is energy both good and bad. We can be sitting at home and randomly feel sad, excited, or nervous. This can be caused by a spirit from the other side coming down into our space. We all have spirit friends who are with us on a daily basis. This is why as an empath, walking past someone you may feel dizzy, angry, nervous, happy, or filled with love. You are simply picking up that person's energy. Some sensitive people can sit in a chair and energetically pick up the emotions of the person who sat before them. If you are touching people all day in your profession, such as a massage therapist, you may need to be mindful of this and cut chords at the end of your day. Giving your energy should strengthen you and it is good karma, but set an intention to dissolve the negative energy that comes your way. A salt bath is an effective way to neutralize negativity. Having a strong sense of empathy is a gift. To have the ability to understand and feel at a deep level creates better healers, better influencers, and more compassion.

We all know someone who has drama that follows them. When you talk to this person over the phone or see them in person. You may feel as your energy is drained as well. You could develop a headache or go home and take their issues with you.

In order to protect yourself from having outside energy come into your bubble there are a few things in which you should do to keep yourself safe. Crossing your arms or legs helps (although it may seem rude to others). By crossing your arms or legs you are cutting off the energy flow. This blocks outside energy from coming in. You can also imagination mirrors facing outwards surrounding yourself. This way other people's energy will bounce off the mirror and go right back to them.

Live everyday one day at a time. Have faith that everything will work out, because everything always does. Trust that life is working for you and in your favour.

CHAPTER 17

Future

WHEN IT COMES TO seeing one's future, you think I would be interested in my own. I would rather keep things a surprise and allow the choice of my future to be up to spirit. If they wish to show me something that will help me along my life journey, then I allow it. Otherwise I wish not to see. I have been shown a few things about my future, such as the house in which I will live in.

I also get told who to trust with this information, along with what to share. The craziest vision of my future was seeing myself pregnant. I was sitting in a living room space on a brown coach. I was watching tv and had my cell phone beside me. The bathroom was 6 steps away from me. My Husband was at work. I was so huge that I could not get myself off the couch, I had to consistently pee all the time. I called my mom to come over to help me, along with asked her to bring me a burrito. I was craving Mexican food and French fries all the time. Thankfully my mom lived fairly close to me. She helped me get off the couch, so I could waddle to the bathroom. My belly was so huge that I could not see my feet unless they were up on the table. Let me tell you I had some seriously fat ankles. My spirit guides laughed when I said I didn't want that! They said not to worry because they will be with me every step of the way.

I had another vison a week or so after this one. I was driving in the car with my husband. We were on our way to get French fries when I got a phone call. I was told I was having twins. My Husband and I both were very happy. Twins run in my family along with his, so we both already were expecting to have twins.

I was able to see what my kids looked like when they were 5. I was living in a log house which was surrounded by trees and green grass around the property. I had a gate in front of my house, along with a gravel drive way. I have been brought to this house twice. Once I was only able to see the outside. I was not able to walk inside. I was playing in the yard with my two kids one girl one boy. My husband was standing on the porch and yelled for us to come in for

dinner. I was so far out with my kids that I could not see exactly what he looked like. I was able to see he was white, tall and fairly skinny. The second time I was brought back to this house I was able to open the front door. I walked in and to my right was the living room, the brown couch from my other vision was there, along with a tv, and my kids playing on the floor. From the living room you could see into the kitchen. Which had a deck and huge windows. My husband was in the kitchen cooking. The upstairs staircase was straight ahead as you first walked into the house. Beside the kitchen was a hallway which lead to a bedroom which was my office. On the wall in the kitchen were family photos. I saw my mom with my children she looked to be about 60. I saw my sister in a few photos, she looked to be mid 30s. I saw my grandma with them too. I also knew some of my loved ones had already passed and they didn't get the opportunity to know my kids.

    I have been shown and told from my guides that my sister and I will drift apart and not be as close. She will move far away from me and my family. My mom will always be really close to me and will end up living with me when my kids are older. I have seen myself living in many different houses. In my near future I will be building a house with my parents in which they will live on the property and I will be living down the street.

With all the information that gets shown to me I believe it is a way to prepare myself. Such as my sister moving far away. I am meant to enjoy the time that I have now with my sister and make time to spend with her. When it comes to moving, I will be moving into many different houses. I assume I will be buying and flipping houses.

At this point the future is very unknown. We can make different choices in which will lead to a different outcome. Our future is not set in stone.

CHAPTER 18

Dimensions

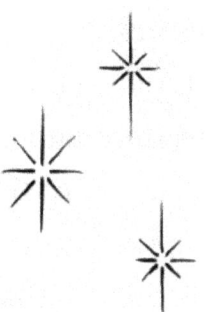

THERE ARE MANY DIFFERENT dimensions in the world. This is to separate us from our physical being. I believe and have been fortunate enough to see first-hand that our souls live on. We never truly die, we simply just move on to another dimension.

When we pass over and go to the new dimension, we are able to come down to earth to visit. We can leave messages for our loved ones, or simply come speak to them in a dream. We receive so much love when we are on the other side, it is a sort of love like no other. There is no hate, no ego, no judgement. Just love and light. The energy is very different from earth. Sadly, here on earth we vibrate much lower and experience too much hate and judgement for each other.

We all have a guide who is assigned to us before we come down to earth. Our guide stays with us until we leave earth. They were assigned to us specifically because they have already gone through a similar life path. We can have guides who are animals, ancestors, fairies, majestic creatures, or even emperors. Animals play a big role in life. Each animal soul has a different meaning and representation. A lot of the times we will not be aware of the signs that are right in front of us. A sign can be anything from a certain bird we see all the time, or a dragon fly that comes to our kitchen window. I still see bears when I need courage. Anytime I see any animals the meaning is always relevant to what is going on in my life.

Besides having a main guide who is assigned to us for this lifetime we also have other guides that will come and go. They come for reasons and seasons. My sister started university and I noticed a new guide joined her team. She was dressed in a business suit, hair in a bun and glasses. She was there to help with her studies. I have also seen a young girl join a friend of mines team of guides with the purpose of restoring innocence and joy. Once they fulfil their purpose they move on. When I started writing this book I had Jacques join my team. He said he was here to help me write. He has a moustache that curls up and a French accent. It should be a comfort to all of us to know our creator sends us so much support and love. We are never alone, they are waiting for us to call on them and lend a hand.

We get to choose how our life goes on the other side. It is forgiving and you will not feel any judgement whatsoever. You will have a deeper understanding of your actions on earth and you can choose to return and learn more. We always have choice and many find peace but some can still hold on to bitterness and even anger. There are different places for us based off what we choose. If we are not ready to pass over and let go we do not have to, although it is suggested we do.

Everything is energy even on the other side. In the physical world we can feel as if someone is following us even when there is nobody there. We can sense and feel if something is a good energy or not. There are some sprits who are not the kindest. They may seem good one moment and then they can be sinister the next. Since the energy on the other side moves at such a fast pace, it can be hard for our guides to protect us at all times. I have been exposed to both so I could learn to discern purity and vibration.

Our world is full of people who are negative, energy suckers, along with positive and up lifting people. In our everyday lives we come in contact with so many people; all who operate on a different energy field and emotional level. Just like on the other side there are many different energies and energy fields. Our intuition is great for revealing intentions.

Our guides are constantly guiding us and protecting us. Allowing us to meet new people in order to better our soul path, or to keep us on our soul path. It is very common for our loved ones who have passed over to be in our energy field, and with us during our everyday lives. They may leave us signs such as a song playing on the radio, leaving something for us to find on the ground, or hearing a voice inside your head telling you to drive to a certain place.

CHAPTER 19

Parents

WE ALL HAVE SOME sort of parental figure. Someone who looks after us and cares for our well-being. Being a parent can be hard and challenging, looking back on my life I realize this. When you are a kid you are care free, make crazy decisions and choices. We just don't listen to our parents. My parents did the best they could with me. My mom was very helpful as far as researching and being patient with me. She would try to understand how I was feeling and took me to many counselling sessions.

I went to countless numbers of counsellors, therapists, and even tried hypnosis. None of them worked. I would feel worse than I did when I showed up. At the end of each session my anxiety, depression, and PTSD were still there. I would still get haunted and could not focus.

I was an angry child, anyone would be if they couldn't physically sleep and were always paranoid. I had trouble focusing on everyday tasks. I lost myself and my mind. I was alone, and I felt it. I isolated myself, I did not want to talk to, or see anyone. I shut out my friends and family. Not only was my life a mess but also my sister's life was limited due to my current situation. It was hard on her.

My parents would worry about me and feel helpless, as any parent would. I never felt more alone as I did in those years of mental health. I know my parents tried to understand what I was going through, but they didn't fully get it. I didn't think anyone could get it. My parents did not respect or understand me and what I wanted. I wanted to be left alone, and not asked how I was doing all the time.

Depression is a funny thing. You want to be alone but you don't want to feel alone. It is a deep dark hole in your stomach. Your brain fills with sad emotions and all you want to do is cry. You don't want to get out of bed, eat, get dressed, see, or talk to anyone.

Anxiety on the other hand is a totally different emotion. For me it was more social anxiety. I would feel a deep sense of panic when I left my house or when there were guests over at my house. I would have trouble breathing, my hands would sweat, I would begin to feel dizzy, my heart would race, my legs would go numb, and my thoughts would race.

PTSD stands for post-traumatic-stress-disorder. I struggled with this disorder and it was strange for me to have. Due to the traumatic bullying I received in school I developed PTSD. I was living my own nightmare because of it. I was unable to sleep. I would have flashbacks play in my mind like a movie. The flashbacks were of situations where I was bullied. I was dysfunctional because I would have these flashbacks day and night.

CHAPTER 20

Roller Coasters

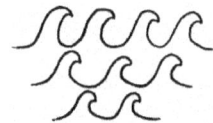

MENTAL ILLNESS DOES NOT define you. We all have our own struggles that we face on a daily basis. It's like we are standing in front of a mountain, deciding if we should climb and conquer our emotions and fears, or if we just stay in one place looking up staring and dreaming about the things we want so badly.

What might be easy for you; may be a struggle for others. We can't judge or measure struggles. We are all fighting our own battles. We have our armour on to protect us. Knowing when to let your armour down and trust is important. I find at times I still wear my armour for protection. In the back of my head I have this fear that I will get hurt again. I know deep down that I will not, I know I am safe. The mind likes to play tricks on us. Even though fear is just an illusion our

body still reacts like it is a real threat. Our brain is ancient and wired to protect us from danger so our species will survive. When it comes to mental health our brains are not user friendly. Fear and depression triggers acute awareness. That awareness will cause you to see things worse than they are instead of better. The brain is on high alert for danger and when you are triggered to focus on danger, you will naturally find it. That means that rope in the grass may seem like a snake. It will over-exaggerate the fear, so be aware of this malfunction. Redirect the patterning. I had to understand my recipe for anxiety and then I created a new one.

Life is a roller coaster with a series of ups and downs. Our life has seasons just like the earth has its seasons. Fall can literally be about falling and failing. It is a time of mistakes and learning. It is shedding unwanted beliefs we have about our circumstances and ourselves. It is a time of questioning who you are and what you are about. Like a naked tree, fall is a time to be vulnerable and honest with yourself and seek the truth. It is about dropping the masks we been hiding behind and discovering our full potential and greatness.

Now winter sucks! It is cold and dark. Depression always takes place in a spiritual winter. Everyone has winter periods where they are down and out, plans haven't worked out and they are being tested. Every season provides learning and

the winter reveals our darkest thoughts and stories about how life should be and it isn't. These negative thoughts can become habitual if we don't challenge them. So we must challenge them because all they are is a bad moment, that turned into a bad story, that turned into a bad movie that we need to stop acting in and find a better one. *The tragedy is when people hit a spiritual winter and they take their lives.* They believe spring will never come. But that is never the truth. We have to be careful not to believe that winter is forever. It is only temporary. Winter is problems and challenges. Problems are not permanent but our soul is. We have to get mentally strong to get through it. You decide the kind of energy and attitude to bring to your problems.

Spring is always around the corner and it is a promise of renewal with buds of creation. It is a time of preparation, such as getting an education. Planting new seeds of beliefs and meanings that will flourish into greatness. Spring has a different energy to it. Faith and trust are born in a spiritual springtime.

Now it is summer baby! We are reaping the rewards of what we planted and worked towards. It's big fun and big enjoyment. We can't wipe the smile off our face because we are dating the person of our dreams and driving the car we can finally afford. It is a time of ultimate freedom, our

worries are small and our blessings are big. By the way, there is a path to a long summer. We ultimately hold the power to create. Therefore, we can create summer anytime we want it just by talking more kindly to ourselves, quieting our inner critic, and focusing on gratitude. We can create our own recipes for happiness and higher states. The quality of our emotions is directly related to the quality of our lives.

Mental health should not be something we are afraid of. Embrace the fact that you are different. You are unique in your own way. My mental challenge has been a blessing in my life. I was able to find myself. I was shown my true power. I was the only one who could pull myself out of the dark space I was in. I had to have strength, faith and courage. I had to realize I did not want to live a certain way anymore, so I acknowledged this and then took action to create change.

Once I found my inner strength I was given the most beautiful gift of all. This was the beginning of being able to speak, hear, see, and know about the other side. I truly believe if I did not go through the experiences I went through, I would not have the gift that I do. I see things on a more positive outlook. There is meaning behind everything.

If you are struggling with anything in your life, be certain that you can get yourself through it. Freedom, light, joy, happiness, everything you ever wanted, you can have. You

will not be struggling forever. I never used to believe in hope or holding on. I never thought life would get better. I went through and experienced my journey. I believe now that things will get better. Find something to hold on to, look for something in your life that is worth living and staying here on earth. For me my dog was a huge role in my life. She was the thing I held on to, she gave me hope, she was my reason to hold on and keep fighting. You are never alone; you have a personal friend who is your spirit guide. You have powerful angels listening to your prayers and offering guidance.

You are on the right path in your life even if it happens to be winter. We have to experience some bad times in order to really appreciate and soak in the good times. You are worth it, you deserve to be here. Great things will happen for you. Spring is around the corner.

CHAPTER 21

Deeper Meaning

OUR WORST MOMENTS ACTUALLY can turn into our best moments with time.

My hearing issues, and ear infections, although they were painful both physically and mentally, it turned out to be a blessing. Without them I would not be able to hear spirit. My eyes used to be a bright blue colour, they changed to a dark green when I was 15. I was very upset over this at the time. Looking back my eyes changed as a preparation for me to see spirit.

I had many mouth infections that resulted in getting my tonsils and adenoids removed. I believe this happened, so I could be a voice for spirit. When you have a sore throat, it is because you did not speak something you should have.

There was a lot of signs I received as a child, I would feel things and be able to pick up things that did not make any sense. People would also tell me that I had great instincts. I now realize it was a lot more than instinct.

I was bullied in school for many reasons. My experience from bullying put me on the path where I discovered my gift. I get to use my experience along with my gift to help others. Bullying helped prepare me for the doubt and hate which comes with having a gift. People can hate on things they do not understand, and a lot of people do not believe in life after death. I learned a lot about myself.

We are all born psychic but not all of us can communicate with the deceased. As we grow older our gifts get pushed down until they disappear. Imaginary friends are usually spirit. I never thought I would end up or be chosen to have the abilities that I do. I was not a Christian, I did not believe in any religion. I believed in seeing proof, before believing in something. You do not have to believe in a faith to receive a gift or to connect with the other side. I believe now in a God, Jesus, and angels. I have seen them and have been able to see things, that I can't even explain. Our world is full of mystery, anyone could have abilities. Any one of us can receive a gift of seeing or hearing spirit. Be kind to one another as you

never know what someone can be dealing with. Spread love to yourself and others. Live your best life, live without fear, enjoy your freedom. Blessings to all.

FOR TOOLS AND STRATEGIES FOR BREAKTHROUGHS IN MENTAL HEALTH PLEASE VISIT MY WEBSITE

www.Peace-of-you.ca

www.ingramcontent.com/pod-product-compliance
Lightning Source LLC
Chambersburg PA
CBHW071501070426
42452CB00041B/2074